Vision Quests

True Stories From The Wilderness

Also by Brad "Little Frog" Hudson

Shamanic Depossession and Other True Healing Miracles

The Truth About You: Who You Are and Why You're Here on Earth

Vision Quests

True Stories From The Wilderness

Brad "Little Frog" Hudson

Little Frog Publishing
Westford, Massachusetts
2014

First Printing: 2014

ISBN 978-0-9908368-1-0

Little Frog Publishing
35 Carlisle Road
Westford, MA 01886

www.LittleFrogHealing.com

Ordering Information:

Special discounts are available on quantity purchases by corporations, associations, educators, and others. For details, contact the publisher at the above listed address.

U.S. trade bookstores and wholesalers: Please contact Little Frog Publishing at 978-590-0186 or email LittleFrogHealing@gmail.com.

For my son, Robbie- May you discover the excitement and wonder of nature one day.

Contents

PREFACE

It was January 2012. I felt a hollowness in my heart that I couldn't describe. Nothing I did could fill that empty spot. I felt like a dog chasing its tail; I knew I needed something, yet I had no idea what I needed.

I asked my guides for assistance. One morning while I was online, the phrase "vision quest" popped into my head for no apparent reason. I knew that when these things happen, it's my guides making suggestions to me. So I googled "vision quest" and clicked on the first website that appeared-www.questforvision.com. When the home page loaded on my laptop, and I read through it, I began to cry. That's my signal that I have connected with my higher self, that I have found something of great importance for me.

A vision quest! This was exactly what I was searching for!

I did my due diligence, and checked the other websites advertising vision quests, but I kept going back to the very first one I saw. That one felt comfortable, like an old pair of slippers. Then I noticed it was based out of Vermont. Perfect! Right down the road from me in Massachusetts.

I sent an inquiry via email, asking if I could stop by for maybe thirty minutes to ask questions about the quest. I received a fast reply giving me a date and time. I appeared on the appointed day at the appointed time, and had a wonderful conversation with a gentleman named Sparrow Hart. He answered my questions and gave me sound advice. I knew I had the right man to guide my quest.

My wife wasn't happy about it. Here I was, 54 years old, going into the Vermont wilderness by myself for four days and nights, without food, a phone, or even a tent. Sure, I was an Eagle Scout, but the last time I went camping was 1973. "What if you get attacked by a bear?" my wife asked. "What if you get hit by a bus?" I replied.

Sometimes you just have to do what you have to do. I knew I needed this. I wasn't quite sure why, but I had learned by this point to follow my intuition, because that is my higher self speaking to me. I was learning to think with my heart, not my mind. And the heart is never wrong.

After I successfully completed the Vermont quest, I swore I would never do it again. It was the most difficult experience of my life. It was also one of the most worthwhile experiences of my life. However, I never expected to repeat the event.

Fast forward two years to January 2014. I had retired from my company so I could pursue my spiritual healing and teaching business full time. I felt great about everything, but something was missing. Again, I heard the phrase "vision quest". Again, I was led to Sparrow's web page. This time I wanted a new adventure. Utah in May- perfect, I thought! My first quest was in the Vermont wilderness, and this one will be the high desert of Utah. Utah will be the exact opposite of Vermont- just what I needed!

And once again my wife was dead set against it. "What about the rattlesnakes and scorpions?" she asked. "What about the snakes and coyotes on our property?" I replied. My point was that I wasn't going to be swayed by remote possibilities. Sure, I could think of a hundred reasons not to go if I put my mind to it. I could also think of a hundred reasons why I should go. Too often in our society we make decisions based on nothing more than fear of the unknown, and we end up missing out on life changing experiences. I told her I was going anyway.

I'm glad I went. It was a hundred times harder than my Vermont quest. I made some incredible new friends there. I had an experience few people ever get. And I returned a better person for it.

I promised my wife I will never do another vision quest. Utah was just way too difficult, and it's still fresh in my mind, since it was only two months ago. But let's see how I feel in two more years...

Brad Hudson
Westford MA
July 2014

PROLOGUE

What is a vision quest? A vision quest is a solitary experience of self-examination in a wilderness setting, without food for a specific period of time. While many cultures have used the vision quest as a rite of passage, the modern vision quest is a vehicle for self improvement, a way to discover answers to personal problems, and a way to connect with Spirit through nature.

A vision quest is a serious commitment. It is a commitment of time and money and energy. The quests I did each required two weeks including travel there and back. Three days of preparation, one day to locate your power spot, four days for the solo fast, and three days' reintegration plus travel days.

A quest can be expensive. Figure around $2,500-$3,000 if you are flying in, renting a car, buying food, and doing a combination of camping and motels. If you are fortunate enough to live within driving distance of a quest, like I was for my Vermont quest, you can eliminate the flight and rental car.

You must be mentally prepared for a quest. You will be by yourself, in a wilderness setting, far from other people. You will have NO distractions- no phone, no television, no music, no computer, no camera, no books, nothing but a sleeping bag, tarp, notebook, and clothes. This alone is a serious challenge. We live in a connected society where our attention span is measured in nanoseconds. This is the most difficult part of the quest because of the incredible boredom that sets in by day three. Minutes seem like years. To put this in perspective, think of a time where your bus, train or plane was delayed by a few hours, and how long that seemed- and that was with distractions! Fasting for four days is child's play compared to the boredom.

You will go without food for up to four days and nights. Water is absolutely necessary for survival for four days, but not food. You may have to retrieve your water from a stream or lake, in which case you will need a filtration system (around $100) to make sure you don't get sick. Or, like my Utah quest, you may have to carry all your water in with you because there is no local water source. Remember, water weighs nearly nine pounds per gallon.

You need a reason for your quest. You may have experienced a life-altering event, like the death of someone close to you. You may need to change some aspect of your life, or change your job. It may be time to start over. Whatever the reason for your quest, your leader will supply you with plenty of tools in the form of rituals and ceremonies to help guide you to the answers you are seeking. I do not provide any of these leader-specific tools in this book because, while some tools, like the Medicine Wheel, are standards, each leader has spent a tremendous amount of time refining their respective tools and thus they are his or her intellectual property. The ceremonies I do describe are generic, well known ceremonies.

I completed two vision quests, one in Vermont in 2012 and one in Utah in 2014. Both were with Sparrow Hart, and both were four day solo fasts. I can honestly say they were the most difficult things I have ever done. I swore I would never do another one after Vermont, but I did.

What follows are the stories of each of my quests.

CHAPTER ONE-
VERMONT VISION QUEST: PREPARATION

The drive to the small town in Vermont where we all met was a short one, only two hours door to door from my home in Westford, Massachusetts. It was 9am on a beautiful, clear Monday morning in mid-September as I pulled into the parking lot of the convenience store right off the interstate. As promised, there was a group of people gathered around an old picnic table. These were my fellow questers.

There were six questers plus our leader. We were all from the Eastern side of the country- Massachusetts, New Hampshire, Ohio, Louisiana, New York. We ranged in age from the mid-20s to mid-50s. Three men and three women, ready to brave the perils of nature in order to find the answers we were seeking.

After introductions, we caravanned to a local campground and set up our tents. This was our home for the next three days, our preparations base. In between time spent getting to know each other every day, we also listened to our leader instruct us on everything we needed to know to stay safe, including setting up a tarp, local wildlife concerns, and first aid procedures. We were also shown how to incorporate various rituals and ceremonies into our quest. Our training was complete by the end of the third day.

The morning of Day Four we packed for our Quest. Most of us took the bare minimum needed to survive four days and nights alone in the wilderness. A sleeping bag, ground cloth, tarp, warm clothes, and a water filtration device completed our pack. We loaded our vehicles for the two hour drive to one of the many lakes in the Green Mountain National Forest. After an hour of real roads, we cautiously proceeded along many miles of unpaved roads for another hour until we parked our vehicles in a dirt area far from the nearest sign of civilization.

We donned our backpacks, and hiked about three miles through hilly terrain into our base camp area on the shore of a large lake. The weather was warm, like Indian Summer. The lake was a calm, deep dark blue, and the leaves were just beginning to morph into their autumn color palette. Autumn comes early to this part of the country.

Around noon our leader gave us the basic layout of the immediate area and set us loose to locate our individual "power spots"- the places where each of us will spend the next four days and nights alone, with no food, tent or fire. After some thought, we each slowly set off in different directions, sans backpacks, to locate and mark our power spots.

Standing on the shore of the lake at base camp, I saw a beautiful peninsula jutting out into the lake maybe a mile from me on my left. The compact beach area was surrounded by majestic oaks, and I immediately thought "That is where I want to be!" I hiked the east trail around the lake, and after about a mile I began looking for a path on my right to take me to the peninsula.

I could not find a path to the peninsula, so I attempted to make a path. The first time I swerved towards the peninsula, I encountered a swampy area where I immediately began sinking into the ground like some bad horror movie. OK, wrong way. After another hundred feet I attempted it again, and this time I was blocked by an impenetrable wall of thorny bushes. OK, strike two. I tried one more time, to no avail.

By this time I had wasted over an hour trying to get to the peninsula. I gave up, threw my hands into the air, and cried out to Spirit, "Why can't I get there?"

The answer was immediate. "THIS IS NOT A VACATION!" Spirit answered me, loud and clear in my head. Holy cow, I had lost track of my purpose here. I was trying to go where I wanted to go, not where I was *supposed* to go.

So I stopped trying, and began hiking back towards base camp. I hadn't traveled more than fifty feet when suddenly I did a double take to my right. I thought I saw something move. I stopped and stared into that patch of forest, but didn't see anything move again. I chalked it up to my imagination, and continued back the way I had come. I stopped again after another fifty feet. "Come on Brad, you know better than that" I said to myself. "You need to turn around and go back, you know that was a sign back there."

I figured Spirit drew my attention to that area for a reason, so I had to return to that spot. Upon arrival, I determined the direction of the movement I saw previously and fought my way through the densely packed trees and undergrowth until I was about fifty yards from the path.

Directly in front of me was a very strange tree. It rose vertically out of the ground to a height of six inches, then paralleled the ground in a wide, three foot "S" shape, then rose vertically for two feet and split into two trunks that went straight up. Right next to it was a tree growing in a perfect half circle.

3

I knew immediately this was my power spot. Spirit led me to these two strange trees, I knew that for certain. But with the surrounding trees growing so densely, I had a major problem. Where will I sleep? There was barely enough room within this cluster of trees to lay my sleeping bag next to the "S" tree, and all the dead branches sticking out at the bases of the trees posed a real problem. I asked permission from the trees to sleep there, and for the trees to protect me. My requests were granted, provided I did not break any branches, dead or alive, unless it was absolutely necessary. The trees told me the dead branches served as protection for the small animals. I told them I would do my best to live in harmony with them.

I marked my power spot with bright orange survey tape to ensure I could find it in the morning, and then returned to base camp. By late afternoon everyone had successfully discovered their power spots and made their way back. We determined who in our group was closest to each other, and this person became our rock pile buddy. Our rock piles were our only means of communication for the four day solo. My partner was Mary, and we walked back to our respective spots so we each knew where the other person was located. Then we found a convenient spot halfway between us and set up a rock pile. I would come to the pile every morning and disassemble the rocks, while Mary would come every evening and reassemble the rock pile. If one of us didn't make it to the pile, that was our signal to go searching for that person and find out why they didn't make it to the rock pile. It was about a half mile to the rock pile from my power spot.

When we finished our rock piles it was dinner time. We each brought a small sandwich as our last meal, and we savored every bite knowing it was our last food for the next four days and nights. Sunset comes early in the mountain forest, and we rolled out our sleeping bags under a beautiful full moon. While the days were warm, the nights in the forest were chilly, in the low 30s. We donned ski caps and gloves and climbed into our sleeping bags for a good night's rest.

Vision Quests

CHAPTER TWO-
VERMONT SOLO: DAY ONE

Our leader woke us at 5:30am, just before sunrise. We packed quickly, hefted our backpacks onto our backs, and assembled in the sacred stone circle we built the day before. When we were ready to depart, we stepped into the circle, and our leader smudged us and recited sacred words, ending with a flourish of an eagle feather, thus sending us off on our four day journey. I was the first person moved to depart, so I stepped into the circle, smelled the burning sage, and on the down stroke of the feather, I executed a quick about-face, and marched silently out of the circle on my way to my power spot. It was 6am of Day One.

I stopped about one hundred yards from the circle and pulled out my sage and abalone shell. I had written my own departure ritual, and I performed it at my designated threshold. It only took a few minutes, but I could already hear my fellow questers behind me, on their way to their power spots. I packed away my sage and continued onward to my spot.

While walking, I noticed tiny frogs everywhere on the trail, most no bigger than my thumbnail. Hundreds of these creatures, scattered everywhere. It was tough to walk for fear of crushing one, or two, or a hundred. I began talking to them.

"I'm just like you, little frogs, I'm a tiny human in this great big world, just trying to find my way."

After fifteen minutes of walking and talking with the little frogs, I stopped suddenly and heard in my head the same voice from yesterday. "YOUR MEDICINE NAME IS LITTLE FROG."

Huh? Little Frog? Not exactly the medicine name I was hoping for. What about "Running Bear", or "Soaring Eagle", something a little more majestic? Were all the good names taken?

Then I realized Spirit was showing Its sense of humor. I'm a big guy, bald and built like a defensive tackle. And now my name is Little Frog. Does this mean someday I will be "Big Frog"?

As it turned out, the only animals I saw the entire four days and nights of my solo were frogs and small birds. My fellow questers saw eagles, moose, foxes, snakes, beavers, coyotes, and more; for them the forest was a cornucopia of animals, large and small. For me, the forest was one really big frog town.

I arrived at my power spot around 6:30am. After I rolled out my sleeping bag, I saw I had no extra room. No room above me, and no room at either end. When lying down, the dead branches were inches from my face; I had to put socks over them at night so I didn't lose an eye sitting up. This space was difficult to get into from the outside too. It required lots of maneuvering around branches everywhere. "At least I'm well camouflaged," I thought.

I tried to hang my tarp as well as I could, given the fact that the trees were not aligned in a nice neat rectangle to tie a perfect tarp. When done my tarp resembled not so much an

8

inverted V, but more along the lines of a flat road with potholes. "If it rains, I'm in big trouble," I thought to myself. "I'll cross that bridge when I come to it."

It was very cold at my power spot. I could barely see the sky due to the density of the trees, and I had no direct sunlight. I discovered a large open area about sixty yards away, but it was all swamp and marsh. Because it was in the sun, it was at least twenty degrees warmer there than the forest, but it had one major drawback. The only places to sit were on large, jagged rocks jutting from the marsh. No soft green grass to lie down on and nap, just mud and rocks everywhere (and after four days my butt was mighty sore from sitting on rocks and trees). In the marsh it was tee shirt weather, maybe 70-75 degrees in the sun, but the moment I stepped back into the forest it was three layers of fleece weather.

Funny thing is, I accepted the situation almost immediately instead of getting upset or looking for a different spot. I am claustrophobic, and my spot was VERY claustrophobic. Spirit was already pushing my buttons. I was determined to not let it affect me in a negative way. I knew this was part of the plan.

As soon as I got my spot set up with my tarp and sleeping bag, a chickadee came to visit. I had not seen nor heard any songbirds anywhere in the four days prior to this. My new winged friend landed on a branch two feet from me and stayed ten minutes while I talked to it. My mother loved small birds of all kinds when she was alive, so I knew this was Mom welcoming me and telling me she was with me. Then I found a caterpillar on my backpack, a symbol of transformation. I gently put him on a tree so he could hang out with me.

By now it was 7am. Only 96 hours to go, so I dove right into my agenda. I found the perfect walking stick, and spent a good part of the day carving elaborate designs on it until it became my power stick. By the end of the first day I had numerous blisters on my hands from my marathon carving session.

In between carving sessions I worked on my relationships with my father, my wife Karen and our son Robbie. I was angry, I was sad. I cried a lot. I yelled and I swore. After hours of this, I finally sent love to them, forgave them for everything, and accepted them for who they are. Just as importantly, I forgave myself for everything I did, and sent love to myself.

Various parts of my past kept coming up, like movies in my mind, concerning events in my life that bothered me. Things that involved anger, blame, shame, guilt, and all the other negative emotions. I learned that each time this happened, all I had to do to make them go away forever was send each person involved love and forgiveness, including myself, and thank everyone for the lesson. Once that was done, each episode went away. This became my way of housecleaning my past life.

I spent the entire day in the forest, and it was cold, somewhere in the low 50s. My two biggest problems are being cold, and being cold and wet. Spirit was pressing my buttons on the former this day. I wore all three of my fleeces, and still couldn't get warm. I made a trip to my primary water source, a stream about a half mile away, to fill my water containers. Of course I slipped on a slimy rock while using my water filtration device and fell into the stream, so now I was cold and wet. I spent some time walking to give my clothes a chance to dry out from what little body heat remained.

Sundown comes early in the dense forest, so I was comfortably ensconced in my sleeping bag by 7pm. The only problem was, I was not accustomed to going to bed that early, so I was wide awake. I purged more of my past, and thought about my life in general. Around 9pm a patch of tall, thin, blue-white light appeared roughly thirty feet from my head. Obviously this was light from the full moon, but there were no other patches of light piercing the dense forest around me. I silently asked "Orpheus (one of my Arcturian guides) is that you?" I heard "Yes, Brad. We are here supporting you on this endeavor". Right after this the light disappeared.

I met Orpheus only a month before, in my backyard one night. It was almost midnight with a full moon, and I was standing on my back deck enjoying the cool night air before retiring for the night. I noticed a sphere of blueish-white light in the wooded part of my property, about sixty feet from where I stood. Then I noticed two very tall, thin rectangles of light standing beside the sphere. The word, "Arcturians", suddenly popped into my head, and I mentally reached out to them and asked if they were indeed Arcturians. "Yes" I heard.

I asked them to take me to their mothership. Instantly I was surrounded by the type of static that appears on old fashioned televisions when there is no signal. There were splotchy black and white dots everywhere. My eyes were wide open, and I could see nothing but this static all around me. It was fun for about twenty seconds, but then I panicked and asked to be brought home. Instantly I could see my back yard again. I again requested to go to the ship, and again I was surrounded by the static. I lasted a little longer this time, but the lack of reference points scared me once more and I asked to return home. I asked for a name, and I heard "Orpheus. We are always available to you." Then the lights disappeared and I went in my house to bed.

Surprisingly, I had absolutely no fear of sleeping by myself in the wilderness under the stars any of the nights. The last time I went camping I was sixteen years old, and now I was fifty four. My belief in the sacredness of my mission was the cornerstone of my lack of fear. I knew my guides and angels would protect me, and having the Arcturians with me was a bonus. None of the nocturnal wildlife sounds bothered me. Every night I heard the food chain in action with wolves and coyotes killing their prey and the celebratory howling that followed. Surprisingly, most of the night it was quiet enough to hear a pin drop.

I had a soundtrack to my vision quest running through my head the entire four days. The first day it was Phil Collins' song "In the Air Tonight" and the line "I've been waiting for this moment all my life" kept repeating all day. The remaining days it was Cheap Trick's song "Surrender", a very appropriate title.

CHAPTER THREE-
VERMONT SOLO: DAY TWO

Sunrise was 6am. By this point I had been in my sleeping bag for eleven hours, but that didn't mean I slept eleven hours. I normally sleep six hours, so I had five restless hours during the night. Even so, I was glad to see the sun. Only three more days and nights to go!

After performing my morning ablutions, I proceeded to the marsh area to bask in the warmth. I was thinking about what many mediums had told me, that I was destined to be a powerful healer and teacher. As I was pondering that, I heard Spirit clearly in my head. "YOU CANNOT HEAL OTHERS UNTIL YOU HEAL YOURSELF".

That makes sense, I thought. I did more work on eliminating my past. Most people live constantly in their past. Everything they do is predicated on past behavior. The goal is to live in the ever present moment, the NOW, by removing the past .

All morning and afternoon I had realizations about my shortcomings. I thought about being selfish and self-centered. I contemplated my control issues. I talked out loud about my issues to whoever or whatever was listening. I discovered trees are very good listeners and they offer excellent advice. They've been around for millions of years, so their accumulated wisdom is worth hearing.

I did many death lodges and cleared the air with my Dad, brothers, sister, relatives and friends. Again, there was lots of shouting and crying and, after a time, acceptance. Acceptance of them, just the way they are, and most importantly, acceptance of me the way I am.

I kept a written journal for the entire quest, so I took frequent breaks to write what I was doing and what was going through my head.

I had a major breakthrough in the afternoon when I realized that this Quest isn't about grand visions and powerful revelations. Rather it's about working on ME- the internal me and becoming an all around better person. Releasing my past frees me from making the same decisions over and over and allows change to happen within. Forgiving the people in my life allows me to understand their future actions as reflections of themselves, not me. And forgiving myself allows me to unshackle myself and concentrate on my path, not what others think my path should be.

This day definitely felt longer than yesterday. I had no physical activity, like carving, to do today, so I was left with my thoughts to occupy me the entire day. One thing about a vision quest, if you are not comfortable with yourself, being alone for four days and nights will drive you crazy. You need to be best friends with yourself in order to make it through the entire solo time.

I crawled into my sleeping bag again around 7pm. The nights were quite cold, in the high 30s. I wore a ski cap and ski gloves along with long underwear in my sleeping bag. I also had a polyester twin sized blanket I kept on top of my sleeping bag for added warmth.

That night it poured rain. It started around midnight and lasted three hours. The rain confirmed the folly of my tarp. I woke up to Niagara Falls falling on my forehead. The only place the water ran off my tarp was directly over my head. My head and sleeping bag opening were drenched. There was no way around it, I had to get up and re-tie my tarp in the middle of the storm. I was soaked from head to toe by the time I made the first adjustment to the tarp. It took me ten minutes to fix everything. I don't like being cold and wet, and there I was, freezing and soaked. Spirit was pushing my buttons again, but I wasn't going to let it get to me. I removed my wet clothing, climbed back into my sleeping bag, and closed my eyes. That's when the wind kicked in and began driving the rain sideways under my tarp. Now everything was wet, my backpack, extra clothes, fleece, everything but my sleeping bag. My polyester fleece blanket was keeping the rain off my sleeping bag. I summed up the situation, figured the rain can't last forever, and actually started laughing about my predicament. Spirit was testing me. No problem, I thought. I fell asleep with a grin on my face.

CHAPTER FOUR-
VERMONT SOLO: DAY THREE

I woke to a beautiful, bright day. I was lying in my sleeping bag thinking about the rainstorm when I heard noises very close to my head. I rolled over, and there was a huge frog, the largest I had ever seen, sitting there staring at me. I greeted brother frog, and we talked for fifteen minutes, frog to frog. When I wished him well at the end of our conversation, he slowly hopped away. From this point on I did not see any more little frogs, only big frogs. I know big frog came to tell me I was doing well.

I threw on wet clothes, jammed everything I had into my backpack, and walked to the open marsh area. There I laid out all my belongings to dry in the warm sun.

I found a rock to sit on, grabbed my journal, and began writing about what happened last night. Anything to take my mind off the hunger pangs in my stomach. My third day without food, and I was definitely feeling it.

I was also REALLY bored. It's tough to go into the wilderness by yourself for four days with no cell phone, iPad, laptop, books, magazines, or television for distractions. Even fires are frowned upon as unnecessary distractions. The first two days went fairly quickly, but now time was moving very slowly. I felt like I had accomplished nearly everything I came here to do, but I still had two full days to go.

I spent most of the day in the marsh drying out, thinking and writing in my journal. An orange dragonfly joined me at 3pm. He sat on the rock next to me and hung out with me for the next two hours. He never flew away. I know dragonflies are about magic and illusion, so I asked him what he had for me. No answer. But when I got up to leave around 5pm, my dragonfly pal departed too, and I suddenly noticed, no more than thirty feet away from me, on the muddy edge of the swamp, the colors purple and gold.

Now I had been in this area for three days. I spent over twenty hours exploring the entire area, including the swamp and marsh, and I knew it like the back of my hand. I never saw anything but green and brown where I now saw these colors. I gingerly made my way through the swamp to that spot, and I could not believe my eyes!

Lying in front of me were the deflated remains of a bouquet of a dozen purple and gold Happy Birthday helium balloons, tied with twenty feet of purple and gold ribbons. They must have floated away from someone's party and landed here once the balloons deflated. Spirit sent me a bouquet of birthday balloons to mark the death of my old self, and celebrate the birth of my new self!

I gathered the balloons and ribbons, packed my now dry belongings into my backpack, and walked back to my sleeping area. I cleaned off the balloons and packed them away. I changed into my long johns and climbed into my sleeping bag for another long night.

CHAPTER FIVE-
VERMONT SOLO: DAY FOUR

At sunrise a woodpecker woke me banging on the tree next to me, then flew away. I got up, excited this was the last day of my solo quest. I spent some time rearranging my backpack and preparing it for the next morning when I would hike back to base camp. I made a final run to the stream for more water. I walked as slowly as I could and it was still only 7am.

I'm bored. Not just a little bored, or kind of bored, I'm REALLY bored! Last night I felt like I had completed everything I came to accomplish. But now I realize I still have twenty four hours to go. Ugh!

I grabbed my power stick and notebook and headed out to the marsh. Maybe some sun will make me feel better. I found my sitting rock, and planted my stick into the ground next to me, but it hit rock and wouldn't stand. I tried again, on the other side of my sitting rock, but it wouldn't stand there either. Now I'm mad. No food for four days can do that to you. This time I slammed my stick into the ground, and it immediately split in half. Instead of one six foot long stick, I now had two three foot sticks. This was my big memento of my quest, the stick I spent six hours carving, my sacred souvenir, and now it was ruined! I was angry for one second, and then I laughed. I didn't need any souvenirs. I had everything I needed in my head and my notebook. I compromised. I left the bottom half of the stick in my power spot when I departed the next day, and brought the top back, which contained most of my carvings.

The morning just dragged on and on and on. I was tired from not eating, and bored to tears. The minutes seemed like hours. My work was complete, so I was now just biding my time until it was time to return. I played my favorite songs in my head. I wrote out musical scales. I thought about the great meals I've had in my life. Anything to help pass the time.

I realized I had spent the entire quest in a very limited area. I never ventured out beyond my sleeping area and the swamp. By this point I didn't have the energy to explore. I kept thinking about the lake, and how beautiful it looked when we arrived. I knew that my water source, the stream, flowed into the lake, so I decided to kill a few hours by walking to the stream and following it to the lake.

Once I hit the stream I discovered there were no paths following the stream to the lake, so I had to make my own path. This was a pain, but at least it kept my mind engaged, thinking about where my feet will step next. A half mile and one hour later I reached the lake.

Next to the shore I found a large birch tree beavers had toppled. It fell in such a way that the trunk was parallel to the ground and about three feet high. It was the perfect seat! I could sit and dangle my legs like a little kid. After four days of jagged rocks and mossy tree stumps this was heaven! I sat there in the sun for several hours, watching fish jump and birds soar. It was perfectly serene.

By late afternoon huge clouds began rolling in, and the wind whipped up. These were storm clouds, white on top, dark grey underneath. Uh oh, I thought, will this be rain? I was totally unprepared for rain. It was blue skies all day, now this?

I continued to sit there on my log, marveling at the immensity of the clouds.

While I was staring at the sky, one of the largest clouds coming across the lake formed the shape of the Eye of Horus, and it was cavernous in the middle. I was fascinated. I had never seen a cloud so huge and hollow. In the middle of that huge empty space a sphere formed, like an eyeball, growing larger and larger. Then it elongated vertically, and took the form of an enormous Jesus in flowing robes and halo. Next, as Jesus morphed into a formless blob, I saw a smiley face behind him. Yep, the circle with two eyes and grin we all know and love! A few more seconds passed and then my magical cloud collapsed into a regular cloud. The entire event lasted maybe twenty, thirty seconds. I sat there, stunned by what I had just witnessed. As I thought about it, I suddenly realized I just had a vision! I had no idea what it meant, but I knew it was a vision.

I returned to my power spot shortly before sundown. I was still excited about my vision, but I was even more excited that this was my last night. Food in the morning! Back to civilization! Only twelve hours to go!

Those twelve hours seemed like forty nine years.

I tossed and turned all night. I spent hours staring into the darkness. I could not sleep.

Then it was daybreak. Of course, after being up all night, now I needed to go to sleep. I finally fell into a deep sleep for a few hours, long enough to feel slightly refreshed. I rolled up my sleeping bag, untied my tarp, packed my backpack, and hiked back to base camp.

Our leader had oatmeal with fresh fruit waiting for us. I never tasted anything so good in my entire life! I ate slowly, savoring every mouthful, every delicious morsel.

I shared hugs and meaningful looks with my fellow questers. We were all now members of a very exclusive club; after all, how many people willingly go into the wilderness by themselves and give up food for four days? Add the six of us to that list!

CHAPTER SIX-
VERMONT VISION QUEST: THE RETURN

The hike out was much more difficult than the hike in, but we made it back to our cars in one piece. A few hours later, we were back in the campground where it all started. I hadn't had a shower in over five days by this point, and I was tired of sleeping on the ground, so I took off and grabbed a motel nearby. This being Vermont, though, meant that "nearby" was twenty miles. No problem!

Checking into the motel was interesting. After spending four days alone, interaction with other humans seemed strange. I don't know what the desk clerk was thinking about the old, grizzled bald guy in dirty clothes who desperately needed a shower standing in front of him. But then I didn't particularly care, I just wanted a long, hot shower.

I made it back to the campground in time for the sharing to begin. Unfortunately, one of my fellow questers decided he wasn't sticking around for the sharing. He had a tough four days, breaking his glasses, getting sick, and spraining his ankle. He was not in a sharing mood, so when he reached the campground he took off for home. Our group of six was now five.

We spent the next three days sharing our experiences and giving feedback to each other. I was very happy with my quest results. I wanted to work on myself and better my connection with Spirit, and I was able to do just that. The other four people reported positive results too. We all came for different reasons, and we all received exactly what we needed.

The last few hours of our last day were spent discussing how to reintegrate into society. Basically most people do not understand the desire to spend four days without food in the middle of a wilderness area. Modern society is far removed from nature. Aside from the occasional camping or hiking trip, modern man's connection to nature is non-existent. Even your own family may not understand why you need to go on a vision quest. Mine sure didn't understand at all; they thought I was crazy.

I lived in complete harmony with nature for four days. Spirit kicked my butt with cramped conditions, cold temperatures and rain, but I knew they were all tests, and I passed them all. Not eating for four days was the easy part. Being alone with my thoughts for four days was the tough part. But I made it through to the end. And even though Big Frog showed up for me, I know I will always be Little Frog in my great big world.

I told very few people about my adventure. Most didn't understand, but that was OK. They don't have to understand it. It only has true meaning for me. I received the answers I was looking for, and I was happy. It was the single hardest thing I ever did in my entire life, and I swore I would never do it again. Never!

CHAPTER SEVEN-
UTAH VISION QUEST: PREPARATION

I retired from my job in January 2014 in order to pursue my healing and teaching work full time. I was the managing partner of an entertainment merchandising company we started twenty years ago, and I knew it was time to leave. Fortunately I had two wonderful business partners, and they understood my desire to leave the comfort of my company so I could concentrate on helping people feel better about themselves. Next thing I knew I was unemployed and without an income.

I was once again looking for answers. I began thinking of another vision quest. I know, I swore I would never do that again after my quest in September 2012. But, much like the way women forget the pain of childbirth over time, I had forgotten how difficult my first vision quest had been.

I found a quest scheduled for the middle of May in Utah that looked promising. Same as my last quest, eleven days total, with a four day solo fast in the middle. The rendezvous point was Bluff, Utah. My only question was, "Where the heck is Bluff, Utah?"

I finally found it in the southeastern corner of Utah near the Four Corners area. It looked like a very small town from the map, the type of place where if you sneeze driving through you missed the entire town. The hard part would be getting there. The closest major airport was Albuquerque, New Mexico, and that was five hours from Bluff via two lane roads. The good news was Bluff was near two major scenic red rock formation areas, Monument Valley and Valley of the Gods. That meant the opportunity to take some great pictures with my new Nikon digital SLR camera.

I booked the quest and the trip. We had a very late spring in Massachusetts, so when I landed in Albuquerque the 80 degree weather was very welcome. I arrived the day before the quest started, so I was able to enjoy a leisurely drive to Bluff through a thunderstorm and two sand storms. I arrived in Bluff too late to enjoy either of the two restaurants in town, so I watched some television and fell asleep early.

I met my fellow questers the next morning at a campground just outside of Bluff. The only amenities at the campground were a water pipe sticking out of the ground for water, and pit toilets. I found an available spot, pitched my tent, and made my way to the spot chosen for our daily circle meeting.

Our group consisted of four men and four women. We ranged in age from 30 to nearly 60. We each had our own reasons for being there. My reason was to increase my connection with Spirit. My shamanic healing practice was taking off, I was beginning to teach classes and I thought I needed some serious alone time with Spirit. It just felt right, and I learned a while back that if it feels right in your heart, it is right for you. Don't worry about the questions in your head, always go with how it feels in your heart.

We all bonded very quickly. We spent the next three days going over logistics, safety, wildlife, rituals and ceremonies. The sun was hot, the air was dry, and the nights were windy and cold. The closest grocery store was 28 miles away in the next town. The closest shower was four miles and cost five dollars-bring your own towel.

On day four we drove out to the base camp site. Base camp was close to the campground, a twelve mile drive, but eleven of those miles were dirt roads requiring four wheel drive vehicles. It took the better part of an hour to drive those eleven miles. We had to keep a few hundred yards between vehicles because of the red dust everywhere. It got in your eyes, mouth, ears, clothes, boots. It formed a fine film over exposed skin. It was nasty.

Our base camp was at an elevation of 5,300 feet above sea level- a mile higher than my home in Massachusetts. Red rock surrounded us in all directions. The only trees to speak of were pinyon pines, scrappy little pine trees that appeared half dead, half alive. They grew to be maybe eight feet tall, and not much for shade, since half their branches are dead. The pinyon tree sap, an amber resin, is used for starting fires because it burns so well, even if wet, and for its healing properties. It can be used to close cuts and draw the impurities from wounds.

Juniper bushes were everywhere. A few cottonwood trees could be seen in the lower elevations. Cottonwoods are an indication water is near. There were no cottonwoods where we were.

What astounded me were all the flowers! I never knew there was so much color in the desert. Granted, the flowers were few and far between, but when I found them they were beautiful. Red, white, yellow, purple, blue, they jutted proudly out of the red dirt anywhere they could. I counted fifteen different flowers in my area. These flowers helped me during a few tough periods of my quest.

Unlike Vermont, there were no natural water sources where we were questing, so we had to bring in our own water supplies. I had six gallons with me for the four days. I wasn't looking forward to carrying them all to my power spot once I found it. One gallon of water equals almost nine pounds.

At our elevation, the road was mainly rock, and there were thousands of long white scratches in the rock. In the late 1800s the Mormons came through this area and used pickaxes in an attempt to smooth out the surface rock and make it passable for their carriages. Every white mark in the rock was the result of someone standing there with a pickaxe, hacking away. What a miserable job!

We went over the layout of the immediate area, a radius of about three miles from where we were standing, pointing out landmarks for navigational purposes. We then split up to find our power spots. Most of us took a few gallons of water with us to leave at our spot.

I was drawn to a large shelf of flat red rock close to base camp. As the crow flies, it was about a half mile from camp, but walking to it took 30 minutes and over a mile in distance. It was a totally exposed area with no place to set up a tarp, quite the opposite of my power spot in Vermont. I was also experiencing some pain in my left foot at this point, so that prohibited me from exploring farther. I found my home for the next four days.

I left my two gallons of water there, and marked the way back with my neon orange survey tape. By dinnertime everyone had set up their rock piles and returned from multiple trips hauling water to their power spot. We sat down to eat our last meal for the next four days. One of the questers brought a watermelon, so we enjoyed that as the last rays of sun disappeared over Comb Ridge, a line of small mountains to the east that resembled a rooster's comb. One of the guys pulled out his guitar and played for a while, and then I played my Native American flute for everyone. By this time the full moon was rising, which was a spectacular sight, along with all the stars you can't see on the East Coast because of the ambient brightness from electric lights at night. We each found a spot on the ground to roll out our sleeping bags, and fell asleep beneath a gorgeous night sky.

CHAPTER EIGHT-
UTAH SOLO: DAY ONE

We were awakened by our leader a half hour before dawn. We packed our backpacks and prepared to leave. This time I brought only a third of the stuff I brought to Vermont, which reduced my pack weight considerably. We all stood around a stone circle, and one by one, as we felt called to depart, we entered the circle for our blessing and then turned and left for our power spot. I was the first one in the circle. With the final downward stroke of the eagle feather, I turned and marched silently away from everyone. The quest had begun.

The sun was breaking over the ridge as I arrived at my spot. I set up my sleeping bag and arranged everything as best I could. I stashed my water jugs under an overhang at the base of the cliff where they would be shaded all day. By this time the sun was blazing, and the temperature rose by thirty degrees instantly. Eighty degrees at 6am. What was I thinking?

I retrieved my sage, smudged my spot and called in the ancestors, angels, guides and light beings to protect and help me over the next four days. I rattled and sang and chanted. I sang the morning sun song to welcome the sun on this new day.

I found some shade by a pinyon pine tree, but I knew that it would be temporary. Little did I know that for the next four days I would be in a constant search for shade. Every thirty minutes I had to move. But I hadn't discovered this yet. I pulled out my notebook and began my journal. My entry at 8:30am reads "Sitting in the sun writing this I can feel the strength of the sun beating down on me."

One thing I had to get used to was the proliferation of biological soil crusts everywhere. These are very delicate living biological formations a few inches tall, black in color, and they are omnipresent. The majority of the area I was in was covered with these formations, which meant careful planning was required for any journey outside of my immediate rock ledge so as not to disturb the soil crust. Something as simple as walking to my rock pile became a frustrating experience in tip-toeing around these formations, doubling or tripling the time it would normally take to walk there. One misplaced step and decades of slow growth would be obliterated.

When I looked closely at the pine tree I was using for shade, I noticed that the tree was half-dead and half-alive at the same time. The trunk split into two sections about two feet from the ground. One section was normal, full of life and sprouting needles and pinecones. The other section was dead, completely dead. Yet the two sections coexisted like it was perfectly normal.

While I was looking at the pine tree, I heard in my head "THIS IS HOW MOST PEOPLE GO THROUGH LIFE." It took me a few minutes to comprehend this message. I finally figured it out. Most people are only half alive; they don't know their purpose in this life, so they stumble and meander through each day. They don't know what makes their heart sing. Consequently they are going through the motions of living, and are basically half-dead. They think their goals are unattainable, or they are just plain unlucky. They don't understand that life is all about joy and love, that we are here to experience good things, and we can manifest anything we want by thinking about it. If you think "I'll never be able to afford a new house," then the Universe will make sure you never have enough money for a new house. But if you think "I want that house" and think happy thoughts about it, the Universe will find a way to deliver it to you. Thoughts are things, they have vibrations, and the Universe's job is to match the vibrations of your thoughts to the vibrations of this reality. You don't have to figure out how to do it, that's what the Universe does. It's enough just for you to think about it, and take a few baby steps towards making it come true, like going to open houses. Let the Universe do the rest. Abraham, the collective consciousness channeled by Esther Hicks, calls this the "Law of Attraction."

The second lesson I received that day happened around noon, when I climbed the cliff wall behind me. It was twenty, twenty-five feet up, and at the top I found the perfect sitting rock. It was a cube about two feet across, and I called it "the throne." The view was spectacular. I could see for miles and miles. I began examining everything around me, and I noticed something about the rocks. From a distance, the rocks around me seemed very solid, very permanent. Yet close up these same rocks were layered, and quite fragile. It was actually all falling apart. The red rock was in layers, and they peeled apart easily, which created the soil from which everything grows.

Many people are just like this red rock. They have a hard exterior over a fragile interior. Our modern society says you have to be tough to make it in this world, that you are only successful if you have lots of money, a big house, and new cars. But this doesn't guarantee happiness. Happiness is not measured by material acquisitions, it is a state of mind. It's doing what you love. It's being in the moment and letting the Universe provide for you. Most people don't grasp this. They work their butts off to achieve what society has told them will bring them happiness, but when they get there they feel empty and cheated.

That is because they didn't follow their heart, they didn't do what they truly wanted to do.

My left foot was really bothering me. When I packed for this trip, I brought my lightweight hiking boots instead of my regular boots. I hadn't worn my lightweight boots for about seven years, but they still fit fine when I tried them on prior to leaving. I couldn't figure it out. Every step was a new adventure in pain. Sitting on my sleeping bag, I cried out "What's wrong with my foot?". I immediately heard in my head "TAKE OFF YOUR BOOTS." Um, OK. I removed my boots, and the bottom of my left sock was covered in blood.

"Oh, no, this can't be good," I thought.

I looked inside my left boot, and found a small nail sticking up through the sole. I had been wearing these boots long enough for the nail to have created a dime-sized hole in the ball of my left foot. That created a major problem for me, because my first aid kit consisted solely of band-aids. I had no antiseptic to treat the wound, but I remembered that pinyon pine resin can be used to treat cuts. I thought about it for a while, and, since I was going to be out there alone for three more days, I decided to try the resin.

I gathered the cleanest resin I could find from the branches of several pine trees, rolled it into a ball,, and pressed it over the cut in my foot. I put on a fresh sock, said a prayer, and put on the only other footwear I had with me- my topsiders. I had nothing with me to remove the nail in my boots, so I was now wearing boat shoes for the remainder of my quest. There's got to be a joke in there somewhere I thought, but I wasn't really in the mood to find it. I just wanted my foot to heal properly.

Sundown came around 8pm. I laid in my sleeping bag, thinking about the day. I drank plenty of water throughout the day, well over a gallon. Hunger wasn't an issue. The hunger pangs would come and go, never lasting for more than ten minutes. Finding shade was a challenge given the area I selected for my power spot. It meant I was always on the go. I had to move as the sun moved, so every thirty minutes I had to find a new shade spot. Thank goodness I had my Thermarest sleeping pad with me. I carried that with me everywhere I went because the rocky soil wasn't very comfortable without it.

I thought about why I hadn't seen any animals during the day. That led me to formulate Brad's First Law of the Desert-conservation of energy. Move only when necessary. Whatever you would normally do during the day, you can do at night when it's cooler. It made perfect sense to me, but I still didn't see or hear any animals during the nights. Maybe the Second Law of the Desert is to avoid all people you find in the desert because they are crazy.

The lessons I learned today were very relevant for me. These are the types of people who are my clients, and I need to understand them, their fears and how they think. Spirit showed me powerful metaphors so I can better relate to them and help them understand themselves in a more productive way. Everyone is unique, but their problems are universal.

The sky was clear and the stars were everywhere. At home, I can see the major constellations, and that's it. Too much ambient light from street lights, parking lots, and the rest. Out here was much different and reminded me of what the night sky was like fifty years ago when I was a kid. The sky was flooded with stars. The moon rose at 10pm, and it was magnificent! It was a full moon, and it was so bright I didn't need a flashlight at all during my quest.

I fell into a deep sleep. I made it through Day One.

CHAPTER NINE-
UTAH SOLO: DAY TWO

I woke with a start. Did I hear motorcycles? I sat up and looked around. That deep, guttural growl of a Harley Davidson I thought I heard was in actuality a group of hummingbirds! The hummingbirds here were much larger than their Eastern cousins, and the noise from their wings sounded like motorcycles. I half expected to see each of them wearing their colors on tiny matching denim vests

My biker hummingbird friends hung out until they were sure I was awake, then flew off. As I sat there watching them, I wondered what is hummingbird's lesson for me? Hummingbird is a hard worker and super fast. He can make incredible maneuvers instantly. Watching hummingbird is like watching an aerial ballet. How does this apply to me?

I move between many worlds, many realities in my role as a shaman. I need the ability to move between them easily, to effortlessly switch directions in a heartbeat as the hummingbird does. I move between this world and the Upper and Lower Worlds, from ordinary reality to non-ordinary reality, from the world of the dead to the world of the dead but not departed. I can best serve others by improving my ability to travel to and between these worlds quickly and efficiently.

I checked my foot injury. When I peeled my sock from my foot, the resin came off with it. The hole in my foot was completely clean! The resin did its job. When I applied the resin, the wound was nasty and filled with pus, but now it was white and clean. I applied a band-aid and replaced my boat shoes. My foot was good to go!

Having conquered my medical issue, I was feeling adventurous, so I went exploring. Everywhere I went, I always had a gallon of water with me. I scooped up my water, along with my flute, notebook, and rattle, and off I went. I went uphill and after thirty minutes I came to a huge cliff. The rock wall itself was about a hundred feet tall. What made it interesting was the bottom had been carved out by erosion, forming a large shallow room. This room was about thirty feet wide, twenty feet deep, and twenty feet high. At the entrance to the room someone had built a large fire pit, using many of the boulders that lay everywhere for the pit itself and for seats around the fire pit. I immediately named this place the "theater", because that's what it looked like.

There was vegetation growing downward from the ceiling by the back wall of the theater. I noticed birds flying in and out, going to the same little bowl shaped crater up on the wall. I climbed up to look, and the bowl was full of water that was dripping very slowly from the rock above. I wondered how the wildlife got its water, and here was a prime example. A tiny oasis in the middle of a world defined by heat and red dust.

As I stood there, hummingbird appeared again, drank from the water, and then flew toward me and hovered in front of me at eye level, two feet away. This lasted about thirty seconds, then he went to drink again. While drinking I heard this strange noise, and I realized he was talking! I had never heard a hummingbird's song before. It was a twittering, chirpy sound. He hung out for another minute, then flew off.

I had my rattle with me, so I sat down, began rattling, and conducted a shamanic journey to the Lower World to see if hummingbird has another message for me. I used a new route down to the Lower World through a hole in the ground I saw near my sleeping bag. As I traveled down the hole, I noticed the walls were covered with petroglyphs. At the bottom of the tunnel I climbed down a ladder, opened the door, and there was a huge, six foot tall hummingbird waiting for me.

"I've been expecting you," said the hummingbird. "Your life will be moving fast, and you will need to travel between worlds very quickly. Call on me for help." And with that he disappeared. I returned to our world, the Middle World, the way I came.

Around noon I walked out into the sun with my digital thermometer. It broke when it hit 115 degrees. The heat was brutal. No wind at all; the air was perfectly still. I drank a ton of water, because the air sucked the moisture right out of me. Now I understood the true meaning of the word "siesta".

As the day progressed, the shade line slowly crept forward from the back of the theater, to where it covered the fire pit. At that time, I decided to do a "letting go" ceremony for my negative personality traits. I wrote each one on a slip of paper. I selected one at a time, addressed the issue out loud for the world to hear, and then burned each paper while saying goodbye to the issue written thereon. When I completed the ceremony, I thanked Spirit, and played my flute. It felt very powerful.

By late afternoon, I was starting to hallucinate. The heat, combined with no food for two days, made me lightheaded. I was going in and out of ordinary reality. Everything began to look different. Rocks and trees were changing shape. I saw faces in everything. My power animals were with me, so I knew I was protected and safe. Maybe this is what hummingbird was talking about. I wasn't hallucinating, merely traveling between worlds.

I sat still, and allowed my thoughts to drift. Right away I was somewhere else, like a parallel universe. Everything was different. I was in an environment I didn't recognize, doing things I didn't understand. Every time I changed my thoughts, everything else changed. During this entire experience, I kept hearing "BE OPEN AND ALLOW'. "I can do that," I thought.

Just before evening the wind picked up and clouds came rushing in. Dark clouds, and all I could think about was rain moving into this area. The weather forecast prior to the solo was sunny skies for the entire week, with no mention of any storms. I was in a precarious situation, being fully exposed on the rock ledge. I found a protected area to stash my backpack in case of rain, and climbed into my sleeping bag so it didn't blow away. The wind velocity continued to increase past sundown, and red dust was flying all around. It made for an incredibly beautiful sunset, with streaks of pink and red and orange and purple throughout the sky.

The wind howled for most of the night. It finally calmed in the early morning hours, although the clouds remained, obscuring the stars. The clouds didn't bother the full moon, though, and its reflected light penetrated the clouds well enough for me to see like it was daylight.

This vision quest, like my first quest, had a soundtrack. When I arrived yesterday morning, I heard the song "A Horse with No Name," by the group America, over and over. This song, about riding through the desert on a horse, took on a whole new meaning for me. Today I kept hearing the chorus of the Romantics' song "Talking in Your Sleep", which goes in part "I hear the secrets that you keep, when you're talking in your sleep". The desert will suck your secrets right out of you, and turn them to dust before your very eyes. The desert can keep a secret forever.

Vision Quests

CHAPTER TEN-
UTAH SOLO: DAY THREE

The noise and ferocity of the wind kept me up most of the night. When the sun finally rose, I noticed the cloud cover was still in place. Thank goodness! Yesterday was just brutal. Today should be much better, with a breeze and clouds to obscure the sun.

I had a powerful dream last night about the death of the old me. This is extremely important to the shaman, because the vision quest signifies the death of the old self and makes it real. The old me walks into the forest, and four days later the new me walks out.

For thirty-five years, my entire adult life, I was in the concert merchandise business. It was my entire identity, and three months ago I walked away from it completely. Sold my stock to my partners and left. The dream I had solidified that. I was out on tour with one of my favorite clients, and when I arrived at the first show, no one recognized me. I went from person to person shouting "Hey it's me, Brad!" but no one paid any attention to me. Then security came to throw me out, and the guys turned into Transformers, which is the only part I can't figure out. Maybe my dream just needed a little action to make it interesting. But this clearly showed me the end of my career. Closure is a good thing.

I made it through two days and nights so far, but can I make it through two more? I felt bad, beat up, hungry, ready to leave. The desert does that to you. It brings everything down to a level playing field. There is no ego in the desert. It makes no difference whether you are rich or poor, famous or not, how big your house is, the desert doesn't care. Not one bit. The desert sees your ante, and calls your bluff. There is no winning hand in the desert.

I saw faces and shapes in everything now. A giant rock at the theater looked like the face and head of the Thing from the Fantastic Four comics. A row of bushes looked like a row of dancing Kokopellis. A bush above my sleeping spot looked like a bison keeping watch over me.

Everything was so red I sometimes thought I was on Mars. But then I would see a tiny green sprout pushing its way, no, forcing its way up, up out of the red soil, and I knew I wasn't on Mars. There is so much death in the desert, it keeps you from seeing the life. Bleached, dead tree branches populated the immediate area, creating macabre shapes. And amongst the dead branches, flowers popped up, stating their beauty for all to see, and not caring if no one comes. They are fine with that, then they die to be reborn next year.

I've lost the enthusiasm I had when I started my quest. I'm drinking less water now; I can't stand drinking hot water. I'm no longer exploring, I don't have the energy for that anymore. It's all I can do to make it to the theater and the promise of shade there. The only positive was the hole in my left foot was healing nicely.

From the theater, I watched five small birds attack a lone crow and drive it off. As the crow was flying away, I asked it to come to me. It circled around, returned and flew over my head uttering a single "CAW" as it passed over me. Then it flew away. Lesson- there is always strength in numbers no matter who or what the adversary.

I performed two more ceremonies in the early afternoon concerning my future. After that, I positioned my Thermarest pad in the shade of the theater, and attempted to nap. I fell asleep for what I thought was several hours, only to find out it was less than thirty minutes. Time was stretching itself, and then collapsing. I lost all track of time. What seemed like hours were actually minutes. When I was in the groove, what seemed like minutes were actually hours.

I stayed in the theater until nearly sunset. I was beat, ready for this quest to end. One more day, I kept telling myself, one more day.

My soundtrack for today was the Police classic, "Message in a Bottle". I really identified with the island castaway, and I was desperate to throw a message for help into the desert ocean.

CHAPTER ELEVEN-
UTAH SOLO: DAY FOUR

Another tough night. High winds all night long. Cold enough to break out my full face fleece hat and ski gloves. When I couldn't sleep I played my favorite record albums over and over in my head to pass the time.

Today was my son's fifteenth birthday. Happy Birthday Robbie! Wish I could be there to celebrate with you. Actually, right now I would give anything to be with you!

I'm miserable. I have gnat bites all over me. Our quest was timed perfectly to coincide with the hatch of the red cedar gnat, which only comes out for one week a year. I probably have a hundred bites on each arm and leg. My water consumption is way down. I'm too tired to drink, plus I can't drink hot water, and all my water is hot. For some reason I have diarrhea. I have nothing inside of me, but I have diarrhea. I'm covered in red dust from head to toe. It's in my eyes, ears and mouth. My back is killing me. I need a hot shower, a rare steak, and a cold beer. Not necessarily in that order.

I had another separation dream last night marking the end of my old life. In it, all my childhood friends were working at my tee shirt company in various positions, and one of them was running it. He came to me for help and I told him I couldn't help him, that's not what I do anymore. I think that pretty much sealed the deal with my old life.

I really need to drink more water. I had none since 8pm last night. Water is especially important to me because I have only one kidney. I lost my left kidney to cancer last year. So hydration is a real issue for me. But I feel so weak and sluggish I can't force myself to drink.

You can always hear a gnat or mosquito flying into your ear, but why can't you hear it leaving your ear?

Since today was my son's birthday, I decided to spend some time thinking about my relationship with Robbie. That led to me examine my relationship with my wife, Karen. After an hour I determined I need to spend more time with both of them, to do more things as a family. Karen and I have been together for twenty-five years, but we share few common interests. I made a promise to do more of the things she wants to do, and the same goes for Robbie. I will be a better husband and father going forward.

By noon I was toast. No energy left. I made it to the theater with my sleeping pad, and I asked my angels and guides to please, PLEASE make the time go by quickly. I can't take another afternoon of time not moving at all. I was so tired I was able to sleep almost the entire afternoon. Before I knew it, it was evening and time to drag myself back to my sleeping bag.

I crawled into my sleeping bag, and prepared myself mentally for the next twelve hours. On my first vision quest, the final night lasted 127 years, maybe longer. I played a few albums in my head. I thought about my last band, and played all the guitar parts of each song we played in my head. I thought about the steps involved in building a deck. Anything to keep time moving forward. It was sometime after midnight when I finally fell asleep.

CHAPTER TWELVE-
UTAH VISION QUEST: THE RETURN

It was daylight when I woke up. I made it! Four days and four nights without food, by myself in the desert. I did it!

I propped myself up on my elbows, and looked down at my sleeping bag. On the corner of my ground tarp, to the left of my head, not eight inches from where my head had been all night, was a tiny scorpion, about an inch long. I grabbed a stick and pushed him away from me. His tail curved up but he stayed where he was, now about two feet from me. He watched me pack up from that spot. That was my closest brush with danger during my quest.

I threw everything in my backpack, struggled into it, adjusted the belts and straps, and set off for base camp. A half hour later I came across our vehicles and dumped my pack besides my truck. I was the second one in. I grabbed some fresh fruit that our leader prepared for us, and settled into my folding chair. That was the tastiest fruit I had ever eaten. I remembered I left some oatmeal raisin cookies in my truck, so I grabbed them and passed them around as each person trudged back to base camp. By 10am we were all back.

We jumped into our vehicles and drove off, headed back to the campground. The drive, difficult on a good day, seemed to take twice as long this time. An hour later we finally made it to the hard road, and ten minutes later we were back in the campground.

I wasn't going to spend the next three nights in a tent though. I made up my mind about that before my quest was barely started. I headed back to Bluff to grab a motel room, a hot shower, and a hot meal.

By late afternoon we were assembled in our circle again. We were all in great spirits, laughing and joking about the things that happened to us. It was great to see everyone's smiling faces.

We spent the next three days sharing our experiences in the desert and providing feedback to each other. Everyone had a powerful quest, but we all agreed the weather and altitude added a difficulty factor for which we were not prepared.

Before this quest I treated it differently from my first quest. My first quest was about losing my past, and working on myself. I thought Utah was about improving my connection with Spirit, but this, too, was about working on myself. Then it hit me, that working on myself does improve my connection to Spirit, and I will always be working on myself. This is a never-ending process of self improvement, and as I learn more about how to improve myself, I can teach others how to do the same thing.

I had no magical moments on this quest as I did in Vermont, but that was alright, I didn't need any. What I got from this quest was exactly what I needed, not what I wanted. The environment kicked my butt both physically and mentally. I performed the ceremonies and rituals that I needed to perform. As a bonus I learned about survival first aid.

This was the single most difficult thing I have ever done in my life. I will never do it again. This quest made Vermont seem like a walk in the park. I can't emphasize enough how difficult it is to be alone- completely alone- with your thoughts for four days and nights. We are never alone in our modern society. We have cell phones and instant messaging, so we are tied to one another 24/7. But are these trappings of modern society really a blessing or are they shackles? Ninety six hours without human contact, without television and music and books and phones- well, not everyone can do it. Nor have many people even tried to do it.

I am a better person for completing my quest. Increasing one's connection to nature directly improves one's connection to Spirit. This was a way to slow down the world, to observe nature and get away from the concrete boxes in which we live and work. An incredible diversity of life exists all around us, all the time, yet we barely notice it. For instance, I was shocked when I counted over twenty different types of flowers in the dessert. And if you listen closely, the trees will share their wisdom with you. Plants will tell you their secrets. But you will never learn these things unless you make the effort.

I know I said "Never again!" after my Vermont quest, but after eighteen months I felt the need to do the Utah quest. This time I'm putting my foot down and saying "Never again!" again. And I'm serious this time!

EPILOGUE

Embarking on a vision quest is a major decision and requires a major commitment. It's not for everyone. It requires a considerable time commitment- two weeks, which is the extent of most people's annual vacations. It requires the buy-in of your spouse or partner, and they may have unsubstantiated fears about a quest. It requires specific equipment you will need to purchase or borrow. It requires stepping out of your comfort zone.

Do your research. Investigate the area of your quest prior to leaving. Check the temperatures and rainfall for that time of year. Bring the proper clothing for the environment. Talk to the quest leader about the hike in and out of base camp. Make sure you are in adequate physical shape for it, and check with your doctor about the fast.

Check out your leader and ask for references. Make sure he or she has a solid background in guiding outdoor adventures and vision quests. Ask about possible wildlife concerns and if he or she ever had to deal with an emergency in the wilderness. If your leader isn't prepared, you won't be prepared.

My leader for both quests was Sparrow Hart. Sparrow trained with Stephen Foster and Meredith Little, the founders of the modern vision quest, in the 1980s. He also trained with Sun Bear. He has led hundreds of vision quests all over the United States over the past 20 years. His wisdom, strength, humor, and compassion have helped thousands of questers.

How do you know if you should do this? Examine your reasons for a vision quest. The majority of the people I met on my vision quests were seeking answers to specific questions. One person lost her spouse at a young age. Many people were looking for the next step in their life's journey. Some were looking for a totally new path for their life.

Me, I just knew I had to do it.

RESOURCES

Foster, Stephen and Little, Meredith. (1989). <u>The Book of the Vision Quest</u>. New York, NY: Fireside Books.

www.littlefroghealing.com- Author's website. Lists services available, classes, books.

www.questforvision.com- Sparrow Hart's website. Excellent vision quests. Other programs available.

www.shamanism.org- Foundation for Shamanic Studies website.

www.shamanscircle.com- Nan Moss's website. My mentor.

ABOUT THE AUTHOR
Brad "Little Frog" Hudson is a well known shamanic practitioner, teacher, multidimensional energy healer, bestselling author, ordained minister, and southern style barbecue fanatic. His healing practice, "Little Frog Healing", is located in Boston's northwest suburbs. He has always asked Spirit to bring him those people modern medicine can no longer help.

He resides in Westford, MA, with his wife, Karen, their son Robbie, and their two dogs, Tessie and Rondo.

Also by Brad "Little Frog" Hudson:

Shamanic Depossession and Other True Healing Miracles

The Truth About You: Who You Are and Why You're Here on Earth

Brad "Little Frog" Hudson

Vision Quests

Brad "Little Frog" Hudson

Vision Quests

www.ingramcontent.com/pod-product-compliance
Lightning Source LLC
Chambersburg PA
CBHW031331040426
42443CB00005B/294